A PORTFOLIO OF

FLOORING
IDEAS

CONTENTS

© Copyright 1995
Cy DeCosse Incorporated
5900 Green Oak Drive
Minnetonka, Minnesota 55343
1-800-328-3895
All rights reserved

Printed in Hong Kong (0495)

Library of Congress
Cataloging-in-Publication Data
Portfolio of Flooring Ideas
p. cm.

ISBN 0-86573-958-7 (softcover)
1. Flooring. 2. Floors.
I. Cy DeCosse Incorporated.
TH2521.P595 1995
690'.16—dc20
94-49672

Author: Home How-To Institute™
Creative Director: William B. Jones
Project Director: Paul Currie
Managing Editor: Carol Harvatin
Art Director: Gina Seeling
Copy Editor: Janice Cauley
Vice President of Development
    Planning & Production: Jim Bindas
Production Manager: Linda Halls

CY DECOSSE INCORPORATED

A COWLES MAGAZINES COMPANY

Chairman/CEO: Bruce Barnet
Chairman Emeritus: Cy DeCosse
President & Chief Operating Officer: Nino Tarantino
Editor-in-Chief: William B. Jones

High-quality resilient flooring achieves the authentic look of natural stone, but is warmer and more comfortable underfoot. It provides a durable, easy-to-maintain surface for this busy indoor/outdoor traffic area.

A colorful departure from the traditional hardwood floor, this custom-designed floor has been finished with nontraditional colors of wood stain. The result is a gleaming wood floor that radiates elegance as it brightens the room with subtle color.

WHAT MAKES A GREAT FLOOR?

Floors have more influence on an interior space than most people realize. A great floor is the foundation for the design of an entire living area. It should create a comfortable environment that is compatible with your daily activities. Because floors have such a dramatic influence on living spaces, functionally, aesthetically and financially, it is important to research, plan and make your selections carefully. When it comes to choosing a flooring material, there are a multitude of outstanding options available, each with its own advantages and disadvantages.

Your lifestyle and the function, maintenance and cost of flooring materials are just some of the factors to consider when making your selections. *A Portfolio of Flooring Ideas* features over 150 color photographs of exciting and effective flooring ideas for every room of the house. It includes information on the materials available and advice on choosing and coordinating these materials for results that are both pleasing and practical.

The first half of *A Portfolio of Flooring Ideas* introduces you to the wide selection of flooring materials on the market today and provides useful information on finding the flooring that is best suited for your specific needs. You'll find tips to help you evaluate these needs and compare them with the cost, maintenance, durability and design features of the various flooring materials.

The second half of the book is a portfolio filled with breathtaking color photography that beautifully illustrates creative and effective ways different flooring materials can be used for hallways and entryways, kitchens and dining areas, living rooms and family rooms, bedrooms, bathrooms and outdoor areas.

Whether you're starting from scratch or replacing an existing floor, *A Portfolio of Flooring Ideas* provides the information to help you select a floor that not only meets your needs, both functionally and financially, but one that also looks fantastic.

(right) **Plush, cream-colored** *carpeting brings a feeling of softness and elegance to this formal dining area.*

(below) **Resilient flooring** *beautifully imitates the look of marble and hard wood to create a luxurious floor that would have been very difficult and expensive to achieve with the actual materials.*

Photo courtesy of Loewen Windows

Photo courtesy of Congoleum Corporation

PLANNING

Assessing Your Needs

The floor is the largest element in a room. Used effectively it pulls together other elements like paint, wallpaper, fixtures and trim to create one integrated look that establishes the composition of the space. Begin the planning process by considering your family's lifestyle, the desired effect you wish to achieve and your budget. Make your flooring selection with an eye to the future, as well. Think about choosing a floor with a neutral design, since a room's decor and furniture are likely to change at least once before the floor is replaced.

The most common types of floor covering are wood, resilient sheets or tile, ceramic tile, natural stone and carpeting. The effect can be either rustic or formal, cool or warm, sleek or plush. Each material brings its own unique look and feel to a room.

Marble and other natural stone materials add a feeling of permanence and create a very luxurious and expensive floor. Ceramic tile is usually less expensive than natural stone and is also a durable flooring material. Wood is a traditional favorite that adds warmth and texture to any room. Resilient flooring is highly versatile; it's durable, comfortable, easy to maintain and comes in a range of colors and patterns, from stone look-alikes to vinyl that looks like actual wood. Resilient flooring is well suited for many areas of the house. Carpeting adds softness and warmth but is not as durable as other flooring materials.

Custom coloring *has expanded the dimensions of hardwood flooring. Diagonal stripes in subtle tones add a sense of width to this hardwood floor. The flow of the design creates a smooth visual transition from the dining area to the living area.*

Photo courtesy of ENDURACOLOR Hardwood Flooring Inc.

6

Brightly colored ceramic tiles are used on the floor and walls of this children's play area to create a cheery, easy-to-clean playroom. The larger tiles on the floor provide a smooth, sturdy surface for bouncing balls or coloring in books.

This elegant, yet durable, vinyl floor handles the demands of an active kitchen beautifully. The rich look of the dark green faux marble unifies the different areas of the room and brings a soothing calmness to the setting.

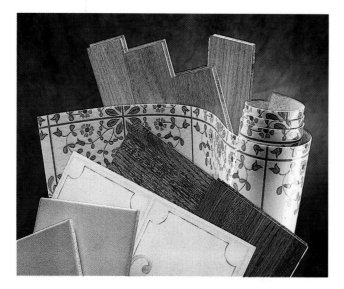

PLANNING
Selecting Flooring Materials

Before you make your flooring selection, visit local showrooms. Collect samples and bring them home to examine in the actual surroundings of your home. Understanding the physical characteristics of the different flooring materials is crucial to making the best flooring selection. Keep in mind that not all types of flooring materials are suitable for all functions. Wood is an example of a flooring material that is greatly affected by moisture; it should be considered for living spaces like bathrooms and kitchens only if precautions are taken to control moisture.

Pay close attention to the subflooring requirements of the various materials as you are researching them, and take the time to check the structure of your existing floor to make sure it's in good condition.

Measure your room accurately to determine the quantity of new materials required. New floor coverings can be installed directly over existing surfaces that are flat, level and well bonded. Damaged, worn or loose flooring can be removed or repaired and covered with plywood underlayment to provide a suitable base for new floor coverings.

The type of materials you choose will affect the amount of subfloor preparation you will need to make. For example, ceramic tile, because it is rigid and inflexible, requires a particularly stable subfloor. When installing a resilient floor, a smooth subsurface underlayment is crucial; a lighter-gauge flexible resilient floor needs a cushion backing, or it will mold to any irregularities in the subfloor.

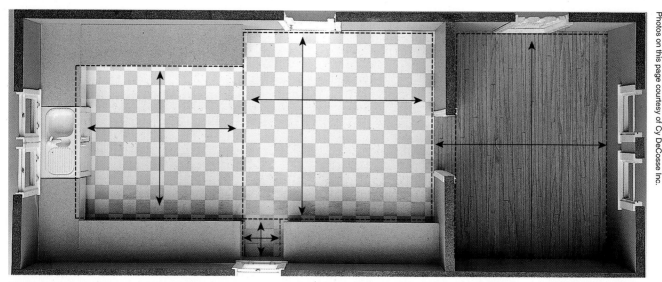

Determine square footage by dividing the room into rectangles or squares. Include areas where moveable appliances are installed. Measure width and length of each area in inches, and multiply width times length. Divide that number by 144 to determine square footage. Add all areas together to estimate total square footage for the entire room.

The warmth and richness of this handsome hardwood floor bring long-lasting, classic elegance to this formal study. The glowing beauty of the wood floor is reflected in the woodwork throughout the room.

Hardworking ceramic tiles combine the durability a kitchen floor requires with the beauty and selection you demand. The nature of ceramic tile allows you to customize your fantasy floor in any color scheme or design imaginable.

Subtly textured blue carpeting establishes the basic color scheme of the room. Visually the carpeting gives the setting a feeling of warmth and softness, while the white furniture and woodwork keep the look bright and breezy. A hint of pattern in the carpet adds interest and helps balance the busy stripes and floral patterns that appear in the upholstery.

PLANNING

Hardwood

Hardwood flooring is an age-old favorite that is still popular because of its warmth, texture, beauty and durability. Rich wood flooring adds a special feeling of permanence and quality to a room. If it is well protected and cared for, a wood floor will last the lifetime of a house and never need to be refinished. Over the years it will look better and better as it takes on the patina of age.

Although generally called *hardwood*, floors made from wood can be made of either hard or soft woods, with red and white oak being the most common species used for flooring. Each species of wood has a specific color range, grain pattern, texture and density—all of these characteristics contribute to the look and feel of the finished wood floor. Wood has a natural resilience, so it is comfortable to walk on and is a natural insulating material.

When considering wood as a flooring material, it is important to look carefully at the room's environmental conditions. Will the room be subject to a great deal of moisture? Water from spills or foot traffic can cause wood materials to stain, warp or even rot if the surface finish isn't moisture resistant. A waterproof finish like polyurethane can protect wood flooring that is subject to water damage and surface abrasions.

The stains used on wood floors have evolved from the traditional golden stain that wood floors have worn for years to a range of finishes, from a deep ebony, to colored stains, to a bleached or pickled surface. The range of options in hardwood flooring is quite impressive. You can even opt for one-of-a-kind custom designs.

Custom coloring *creates a muted green border that adds a subtle but dramatic accent to this hardwood floor and defines the living room area. The natural stone in the entry is an ideal companion for the hardwood floor aesthetically and because it takes the initial punishment of shoes entering the house.*

Nothing brings warmth to a home quite like wood. In this sunken study, the wood theme is carried through from the floor and deep baseboards to the railing and steps leading up to the bookcases—even to the furniture itself.

11

Hardwood floors are available in three basic types; strip, plank or block. Strip flooring is the most common basic type of hardwood flooring; it consists of narrow boards laid in random lengths. Most plank flooring today is very similar to strip wood flooring, except the planks are produced in random widths as well as random lengths. Block flooring, also called parquet, wood mosaic or wood tile, is wood flooring laid in blocks or squares. The blocks may be solid pieces, laminated sheets or squares assembled from smaller pieces of wood. Most wood block flooring is considered a floor covering only, while strip and plank flooring actually contribute to the structural strength of a house.

There are grading systems used for different species of wood. In general, the higher grades are considered the best quality in terms of strength and regularity in appearance. Flooring is milled in several thicknesses and comes in two forms: tongue and groove, which gives a strong interlocking joint that conceals the nails; or square edge, which must be nailed through the face of the flooring and the nails remain visible.

Most commercial hardwood flooring has a long-lasting finish applied during the manufacturing process. Today, finishing options for hardwood flooring include new alternatives such as decorative patterns, stenciling, faux finishes and special paint techniques like color washing.

Photos this page courtesy of Bruce Hardwood Floors

(above) *A busy herringbone* pattern in this hardwood floor is the perfect accompaniment to the detailed architecture of the room. An intricately patterned Oriental rug softens the feel of the room and helps to define the dining area.

(right) *A custom crafted* wood tile floor is highlighted with cream-colored diamond accents. The square block design flooring pattern adds texture and a touch of class to an already elegant entryway.

(right) **Simple yet elegant,** hardwood strip flooring adds glowing warmth and long-lasting beauty to this formal study.

(below) **A whitewashed,** pickled finish has become a popular alternative to the golden stain traditionally given hardwood floors. This pickled finish matches the weathered look of the other woodwork in the room.

Photos courtesy of Bruce Hardwood Floors

(above:) **The beauty and texture** *of raw wood have been re-created with a soft white finish on this natural hardwood floor. The texture and color created by the grain of the wood becomes the focal point of the room. Furniture and accessories tie the setting together with subtle accents of pastel colors and natural stone textures.*

Alternating grain patterns and *different colored stains used in this wood tile floor create a checkerboard pattern. Small eye-catching accent diamonds add an old-fashioned feel and a sense of uniformity to the setting.*

PLANNING
Ceramic Tile & Natural Stone

Today, ceramic tile is a practical flooring for almost any room in the house. Made from hard-fired slabs of clay, ceramic tiles offer endless creative possibilities because of the almost limitless number of patterns, colors, shapes and finishes available. Ceramic tiles come glazed or unglazed. Glazed tiles may be glossy, semi-matte or dull. Unglazed tiles have no finish; the colors, seen in the body of the tile, are usually earth tones.

Natural stone materials have always been held in high esteem as a flooring option. Nothing is more effective than slate, granite, marble, fieldstone or limestone for cool good looks and elegance. Natural stone adds the feeling of substance, creates a pleasing visual rhythm and brings a sense of scale to the space. For visual and textural interest, natural stone materials remain unchallenged.

Handsome terra-cotta gives a regional southwestern flavor to a home, while brick pavers, with oxblood color and rough texture, have a vintage appeal. A veined marble floor announces sophisticated living, while creamy travertine suggests a neoclassical or natural contemporary style. Irregular shapes of fieldstone for a floor create an Adirondack-style lodge look.

The durability and attractiveness of ceramic tile and natural stone flooring are definite advantages. But the limitations of expense, structural restraints and other practical considerations such as cold and noise, are other factors to think about when considering ceramic or natural stone flooring.

Cool, clean ceramic creates an elegant entryway. The high-gloss tiles have a faux marble finish that complements the marbled walls. Continuing up the stairs and into the living room area, the sleek ceramic tiles carry the distinctive look into the next room.

(above) **Stylized ceramic** tiles have the worn, weathered look and texture of natural stone tiles, but are uniform and more orderly in appearance. A delicate border and subtle design create a separate dining area in the floor.

(left) **A trace of pink** warms and softens the cool look of ceramic in this bathroom floor. The ceramic tile extends partially up the wall, protecting it from water damage.

Ceramic and natural stone share some common characteristics that should be kept in mind when considering them as a flooring option. These materials tend to be cool to the touch, which is an advantage in hot weather, but a possible source of discomfort in cold climates. Because they are heavier than most types of flooring, wood-frame subfloors may have to be reinforced to support the extra weight.

Photo courtesy of Florida Tile Industries, Inc.

Photo courtesy of Color Tile Inc.

The elegant look *of marbleized ceramic helps capture a period of style. Tiles have been cut and laid to resemble rustic stone pavers. The vintage look of the floor matches the antique decor of this bathroom. The pattern of the tiles creates a textured surface desirable for a bathroom floor, and also adds visual interest to the look of the floor.*

*The **uneven texture** and large grout lines in this tile floor create a safer surface in this kitchen. The custom color selection available in ceramic tiles allows a blue tile border to pick up the blue used throughout the room.*

These materials also tend to be slippery when wet, so it is best to choose products with enough surface texture to provide adequate traction. Natural stone tends to deflect sound rather than absorb it, so if the acoustics of the room are important, use unglazed or textured materials, which will absorb sound better.

PLANNING

Resilient

Resilient flooring is entirely man-made; it evolved after the development of resins and synthetics. Linoleum, an early example of resilient flooring, has been largely replaced by newer polyurethane and vinyl materials that are moisture- and stain-resistant, easy to install and simple to maintain.

Vinyl flooring is one of the most dramatically improved resilient flooring materials available today. It offers surprisingly high-style looks, great solid colors and designer faux-finish effects that reflect the current trends in design. Polyurethane sheet flooring has a tough surface that is virtually maintenance free, while vinyl sheet flooring has a top layer of vinyl bonded to a backing, which produces a cushioned floor that is comfortable to walk on, durable and quiet. Inlaid resilient flooring is also very durable; it has the pattern and color running continuously through its entire thickness, so colors are more intense and wear is less noticeable.

Durability, continuing value and low maintenance make resilient flooring a choice no longer limited to the kitchen, mud room or bath. Today you can find resilient flooring in many of the main living areas of the home. Authentic-looking imitations of all types of flooring—brick, slate, wood, marble, terrazzo, flagstone and ceramic—are available in resilient flooring materials. They are generally less expensive than natural-base products, with the exception of inlaid and top-of-the-line vinyl, and are a popular way to produce the look of a more expensive floor, with the advantages of a resilient.

(above) **A sleek,** *custom-designed inlaid floor sets the futuristic tone of this kitchen. This high-style floor is not only beautiful, but very durable as well. The inlaid design, including the pinstripe accents, runs through the entire thickness of the floor—an attractive quality that really endures.*

(below) **Durable,** *less expensive resilient flooring beautifully creates the look and feel of an elegant marble entryway.*

Resilient flooring is easy to handle. It comes in sheets up to 12 feet wide or in 9 or 12-inch-square tiles. The visibility of seams in sheet flooring can be minimized by placing them in secondary areas of the room. You can also hide the seam if you run it along an existing line in the pattern of the design.

Tiles can be laid out in a grid format oriented square to the room or on a diagonal. The pattern can include special borders or even a random design. For both sheet and tile floors, pattern, surface texture and color will contribute to the final look of the room.

(above) **Sheet vinyl** *flooring can be custom cut to create original flooring patterns. The wide spectrum of colors available opens the imagination to a multitude of design possibilities.*

(right) **The weathered** *look and texture of natural stone have been beautifully re-created in vinyl. Sheet vinyl flooring produces a surface that is smooth, clean and durable.*

Versatile sheet vinyl *is an excellent choice for this dual-purpose kitchen and dining area. Textured vinyl provides an easy, cost-efficient way to create exciting floors like the one shown here. A stunning two-tone marble floor accented with metallic gold pinstripes is both elegant and affordable when it's really a resilient floor.*

(above) **The slick, cool look** of ceramic tile can also be found in resilient flooring. With hundreds of new, natural-looking finishes and patterns available, resilient flooring offers an option that's often less expensive, more comfortable and easier to maintain than the real thing.

(right) **Comfortable, less expensive** resilient floors are one way to achieve the bright, clean look of ceramic in this multipurpose room. The flexibility of the floor design allows the room to transform easily from sewing room to guest bedroom. The delicate pattern in the floor is seen even in the fabric on the daybed and the wallpaper.

A delicate art deco design in the flooring keeps this small kitchen bright and bouncy. Textured for better traction, this sheet vinyl flooring is easily cut and installed in odd angled areas, such as in this kitchen.

PLANNING

Fiber

Comfort and appearance make carpeting a popular flooring for living rooms and bedrooms. The performance of carpeting is better overall because of new stain-resistant and wear-resistant fibers. The development of these new hard-wearing fiber materials has brought the benefits of carpet to bathrooms and kitchens. Although woven carpets are still available, most carpets today are made by the tufting process, where tufts of carpet yarn or fiber pierce through the backing material and form the carpet pile. Carpeting is available in wool, acrylic, nylon, polypropylene and polyester, as well as combinations of these materials. Synthetic carpets dominate the market because of their lower prices and easier maintenance.

Plush, shag, level loop and sculptured pile are some of the many styles of carpeting. Plush carpeting has a smooth, even surface that gives the carpet a soft look that has a shadowed appearance after vacuuming. Because the pile is closely woven, the material doesn't crush easily. Shag carpeting has a more casual look; it comes in solid colors, tweeds or multicolored, and in fibers of different lengths. Not as dense as plush, shag carpeting is less expensive but not as long-wearing. Sculptured pile carpeting uses different lengths of pile to achieve a rich surface texture and design.

Carpet with tight pile loops that are uniform in size and height is called *level loop pile*. The tightly constructed loops make it easy to maintain and very durable. Carpet with loops of uneven height is called *multi-level loop*, and carpet that has cut loops and even height is called a *cut loop*. Nubby, loop-pile carpets are commonly termed *Berber*. At first offered only in wool, synthetic Berbers, with considerably lower prices, are now available. Carpet that has straight tufts blended with twisted or curled tufts is called *frieze*. Friezes or twists offer a resilient textured pile that resists matting and does not show footprints. These carpets are also called *trackless*. Carpeting with variable loop piles is the most durable and the best choice for high traffic areas such as halls, stairways or family rooms.

Comfortable wall-to-wall carpet makes this quiet fireside setting even cozier. The soft golden tones in the carpet and the walls give the room visual warmth and complement the beauty of the natural wood and antique fixtures.

Area rugs are an easy way to soften a space and remove the hard edges. A compromise between a hard surface and wall-to-wall carpet, the area rug is a versatile alternative with something to offer in every decorating style. Often area rugs combine different elements in their construction to create unique and different designs: painted sisel rugs with fabric tapestry borders are a widely used example. Busy, all-over patterns are a good choice for area rugs used under dining room tables; spills and stains will mix and blend more easily into a busy design.

Conventional carpeting has no backing and requires a pad underneath. Carpeting with a bonded rubber backing is called *cushion-backed* and needs no separate pad. Both types of carpeting can be installed directly over a well-prepared subfloor or any old flooring that's clean, smooth and free from moisture.

Because the pad cushions the carpet from premature wear and provides comfort underfoot, your choice of pad is as important as your carpet choice. A pad that is too thick may interfere with good balance and be hazardous. A pad that is too thin will cause premature wear of the carpet and may even cause the carpet seams to split. A 6- to 8-pound rebound pad is your best bet for economy and performance.

The subtle floral grid pattern in this sculpted carpeting emphasizes the texture of the material and provides a plush floor for this cheerful setting. The sea of blue carpet is visually balanced by a wide band of blue just below the ceiling.

Plush carpeting creates a velvety background for this elegant study. The rich, luxurious carpet provides a beautiful backdrop for the robust leather and wood decor.

(top left) **An intricately patterned** Persian Serape rug adds softness to the room and defines the sitting area in front of the fireplace. The handsome, polished hardwood floor is the perfect place to display the deep, rich beauty of this timeless treasure.

(top right) **A custom-colored,** braided area rug adds an island of texture and color to the sea of soft beige wall-to-wall carpeting.

(bottom left) **A fabulous French** Aubusson-style rug fills this impressive sitting room with stately elegance. The vivid colors of the rug are reflected in the walls, the window treatments and the upholstery on the furniture.

PLANNING
Lifestyle & Function

The amount of traffic a floor will have to endure is an important consideration in your selection of a flooring material. Some materials are more resistant than others to grease and oil, water, temperature changes, scarring or chemicals. For instance, although wood materials look good in almost any area of the house, rooms that are subjected to a lot of moisture and humidity, like kitchens and bathrooms, are not the ideal environment for wood floors.

Wood flooring is also subject to scratches and surface abrasions. If the area collects a lot of sand or grit from traffic, you should consider using a very dense hardwood, such as oak, teak or beech, finished with several coats of a durable, wear-resistant surface finish, such as polyurethane.

Avoid slippery finishes whenever possible. In kitchens and bathrooms, don't use flooring that becomes slick when damp. Loose rugs laid on hardwood floors should have a nonskid backing or pad.

The way sounds react to different materials will also influence which flooring materials you choose. Soft materials, like vinyl, rubber and carpeting, deaden sound. Wood, ceramic tile, masonry and other hard surfaces tend to reflect sound rather than absorb it. Use unglazed or textured materials to reduce noise.

Natural stone and ceramic products feel cool to the touch, an advantage in hot weather but potentially uncomfortable in cold climates. Ceramic, stone and some resilient surfaces also get slippery when

(left) **New designer** *patterns take color and texture to new limits. You can create exciting, eccentric, eclectic new looks as never before.*

Photo this page courtesy of Congoleum Corporation. Photo opposite page courtesy of Armstrong World Industries Inc.

The rustic theme of this kitchen takes everything back to the basics, right down to the rough, worn look of a natural stone floor. The realistic-looking faux stone design in this resilient sheet flooring is a way to use a reasonably priced, durable material on the floor and still maintain the intended design theme.

wet; choose materials with enough surface texture to provide adequate traction.

The physical warmth, softness and noise-reduction qualities of carpet make it unique among floor treatments. Man-made fibers like nylon or antron are recommended for homes with pets, allergies or young children. One drawback to carpet is that it is subject to changing style and color trends and can quickly date a house.

Wood offers a bit more cushioning than other hard surfaces and its versatile style makes it appropriate for contemporary or traditional interiors. The enduring qualities of hardwood floors can last the lifetime of a home.

Resilient floors are easy to maintain, durable and comfortable underfoot. They are practical, relatively inexpensive, easy to install and can be laid over many existing floor surfaces.

PLANNING
Wear & Maintenance

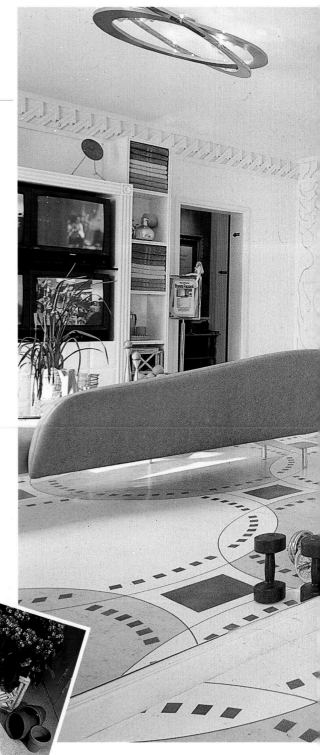

New developments in flooring materials, protective finishes and cleaning techniques make floor maintenance easy. However, flooring that gets a lot of traffic will get dirty and eventually may scratch or scuff. Each type of material has its own maintenance needs in order to keep looking good.

Ceramic and natural stone floors must be sealed when installed, but simple sweeping and occasional damp mopping are the only maintenance necessary. Natural stone materials like slate and marble can be expensive, but they are durable and practically maintenance free. They are hard-wearing, easy to maintain and attractive.

Wood needs a dry climate, so avoid wet mopping and using water-based waxes. You'll get the best wear and appearance by vacuuming or dry mopping wood floors about once a week and waxing the surface once or twice a year. A good wood floor will last the lifetime of most homes, can be refinished several times and will actually improve with age. Older wood floors can be painted in solid washes of color for a fresh look that conceals any scars or blemishes.

Carpeting is a major decorating investment, so buy the best quality product you can afford. Look for one with stain protection built into the product. Regardless of the fiber used, proper care of

(right) ***Durable doesn't*** *need to be boring. With original designs created in tough, resilient materials, you can make a statement that really stays put.*

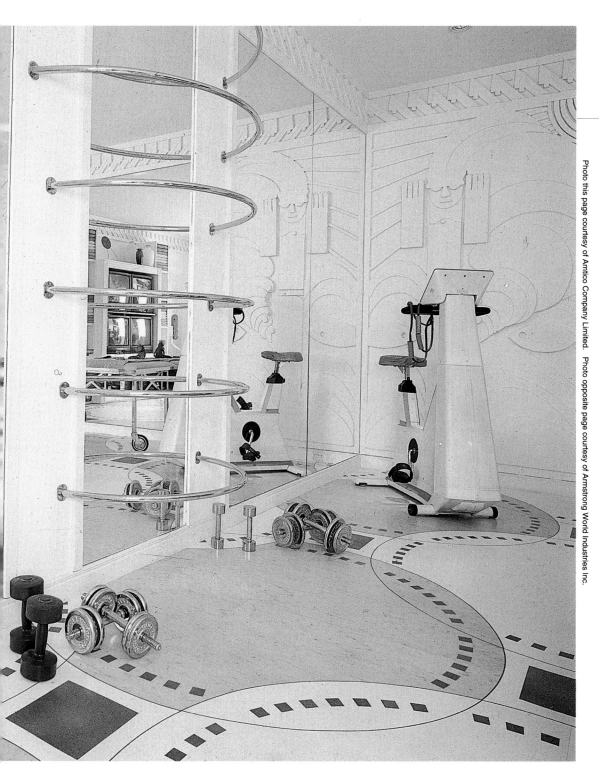

Photo this page courtesy of Armtico Company Limited.   Photo opposite page courtesy of Armstrong World Industries Inc.

Heavy weights won't make a dent in this durable vinyl floor. The surface is more comfortable than the concrete floor of a basement or gym, and you can visually inspire yourself and others with custom designs like the geometric pattern shown here.

carpeting requires regular cleaning. Dirt particles on the surface, not foot traffic, do the damage that wears out the carpet. Grit grinds into the fabric as the carpet is walked on. Neglect can ruin even a quality carpet, while routine cleaning can extend the life of even an inexpensive product. A good pad will protect the carpet from premature wear and provide more comfort, so your choice of pad is as important as your choice of carpet.

Resilient flooring material should have a wear layer thickness of at least 15 mils. Resilient floors with thinner layers may look good when new but will not provide long wear. And unless they have cushion backing, the lighter-gauge resilient flooring will mold to any irregularities in the subfloor. Today's quality resilient products have a surface or wear layer of 20- to 30-mil thickness.

A lustrous hardwood floor is protected and visually softened by a colorful area rug. The rectangular rug picks up the blue accent color used throughout the room and helps define the sitting area. And because area rugs are small and easy to move, everyday maintenance of a hardwood floor is easy.

Photo courtesy of Bruce Hardwood floors

Primary colors set the theme for this fashionable and fuctional vinyl floor. Vinyl offers a unique combination of qualities like good looks, value, durability and easy maintenance, making it the ideal choice for this high-traffic area.

Photo courtesy of Armstrong World Industries Inc.

Custom-colored
wood tiles combine the look of beautifully hand-crafted, detailed ceramic tile with the warmth and richness of natural wood. While years of traffic and wear can take its toll on a tile floor, worn hardwood floors can easily be revived.

Quality hardwood
floors feature some type of urethane no-wax finish to protect against the wear and tear of active families. This lively parquet floor is one of the new generation of hardwood floors that offer distinctive beauty, yet are so easy to care for — simple vacuuming and occasional damp mopping are all that's needed to keep them looking great.

Even expensive carpets can't compare to the long-lasting luxury of a hardwood floor. And the beauty is more than just skin deep; hardwood floors offer some unprecedented advantages, like timeless beauty that's always in style and durable, easy-care comfort.

This custom-crafted wood tile floor is a wise investment; the long-lasting durability of wood means it will earn its keep for years to come. The festive floor tile features an easy-care finish that's tough, durable and cleans up like a dream.

PLANNING

Cost

Each type of flooring material is available in varying qualities and prices. In general, the less expensive the material, the less quality you will get for your money. More expensive materials generally have more durability and will look good much longer than a cheaper version of the same flooring. The initial cost will be repaid over the years with better-looking floors for a longer period of time.

Flooring products manufactured from a natural-material base, like wood, natural stone and rubber are generally more expensive than entirely man-made products, with the exception of top-of-the-line, inlaid solid vinyl products,

which are at the high end of the cost scale for both material and labor. When controlling costs and easy maintenance are the primary factors for choosing a type of flooring, sheet vinyl is an optimum option.

The cost of most natural stone flooring is high, mainly because of the expense of handling and shipping the heavy materials. Moreover, the weight of the material requires a very strong, well-supported subfloor. If you're considering a natural stone floor, check with your local building materials supplier for availability; because of its weight, natural stone material isn't usually shipped great distances.

PLANNING

Aesthetics

Does your floor create the effect you desire? Does it increase or diminish the sense of space in a room? How does it coordinate with existing furniture and decorative style? The aesthetics of a room are greatly influenced by the flooring you choose. If the interior is to be formal and traditional, or sophisticated and contemporary, often a polished stone surface like marble is chosen. A more casual environment can be created by using a stone that has a matte finish. Different flooring materials can even be combined to create interest and drama. Hard-surface materials like wood, marble, tile and stone may be used to define separate areas or to create a special effect by combining one material with another.

In addition to hard surfaces, most interiors also need the softness that is supplied by carpeting or area rugs. Plush flooring reduces noise levels, adds warmth and coziness and cushions areas where comfort is required underfoot.

Color has a dramatic influence on the ambience or atmosphere of a room. More than any other element color has the power to unify the interior design throughout a house. The same color or the same color theme, used in successive rooms, helps to integrate interior spaces—even in a house that combines different design styles.

A light floor, like light ceilings and walls, will make a room look more spacious and open by reflecting more of the available light. Darker tones tend to contract and confine space, but can also make the room appear warmer and more intimate or cozy. A floor that is too dark can absorb an enormous amount of light, making a room look smaller and darker than is necessary. If you have dark stained hardwood floors, for example, a high-gloss polyurethane surface will brighten up the room. A glossy finish will reflect more light than a matte finish will.

(left) **The look of cool, clean white** ceramic tile gives this room a feeling of springtime freshness. The understated elegance of ceramic is achieved with a textured vinyl that is less expensive and more comfortable than actual ceramic tile.

Photo left courtesy of Armstrong World Industries. Bottom photo courtesy of Mannington Mills Inc.

(above) **A classic checkerboard design** *adds a dramatic flair to this multipurpose area. The large tiles visually expand the sense of space and instill balance and continuity between the bright white cabinets in the kitchen and the brilliant yellow walls and bright colors of the sitting area.*

39

DESIGN

As a general guide, good design is simple design, especially when considering the influence a flooring design will have on your interior space. Simplicity isn't always easy to achieve. It requires restraint and thoughtfulness in planning. Pattern, scale, texture and color are all design factors that influence the effect a floor will have on a space.

Pattern and scale work together to make a space feel expansive, calm, lively, busy or cramped. Texture is often an inherent part of the pattern. The shapes that make up the pattern also affect the overall feeling of the design.

The surface finish and color of flooring materials also play a part in a room's design. Rough surfaces look hand-worked and casual. Smooth, slick surfaces look more refined and elegant. The more natural and neutral the color, the more flexible the space will be when coordinating with other design elements, now and in the future.

When designing a tile pattern, remember that the size, shape and surface texture work with the pattern and color of the grout lines to form an ordered geometric grid. The color of the grout either accentuates the grid pattern or minimizes its visibility. The scale of the tile also creates an effect that varies with the scale of the room. In a large room, small units will visually blend together and appear as an even pattern across the floor. On the other hand, large tiles will stand out as distinct units. Because a tile floor is composed of unit pieces, pattern is a dominant aspect in the flooring design. Tiles of contrasting color can be used to set a pattern into the flooring or to define a separate space.

(below) **Tiles of contrasting colors** *can add a note of drama and geometric interest to a floor. Polished black and white marble tiles create a classic, elegant look in this entryway and a dramatic setting for the Oriental theme.*

White, marbleized vinyl squares with cut corners and small black inserts create an art deco look in this striking entryway. The realistic look of the faux marble finish and the diagonal direction of the design add a sense of weight and visual width to this narrow hallway. The subdued scale of the pattern adds interest to the small space without overpowering it.

Photo opposite page courtesy of American Olean Tile Company
Photo this page courtesy of Amtico Company Limited

The realistic texture and tone of this resilient floor give it the look and feel of an authentic stone surface. A fine white grid dramatically changes the look of the room—it lightens the heavy feel of the faux stone and it serves as an anchor that unites the kitchen and dining area.

Flooring patterns, such as herringbone or grid designs, are effective ways to create interest in a long or wide space. Linear materials like hardwood strips make a strong directional statement by creating lines that run either the length or width of the room. A proportionally narrow, long room can be made to look wider and more spacious if you run the strips or planks across the width. On the other hand, wood block or parquet tiles make no directional statement, but do provide a very definite pattern or even a complex mosaic. With both types of wood materials, you have a range of detail options.

The tone and sheen of a finished floor also contribute to the room's ambience. Dark floors with a matte finish can feel heavy and grounded; they tend to contract the apparent size of the space. Lighter, glossy finishes create an expansive feeling of space. When making your selections, think of the overall visual effect or mood you'd like to create.

A contemporary sculpted Chinese portrait rug is the centerpiece of this formal living room area. The soft pastel colors in the rug tie in with other elements in the room to create a subtle Oriental motif.

Exposed wood plugs *in a contrasting color give this plank floor the look of an old-fashioned square-edged hardwood floor. The dark color of the plugs adds a rustic, casual flavor to the setting and enhances the warmth and beauty of the natural wood.*

DESIGN

Color

Color has the power to affect the ambience or atmosphere of a room. More than any other element, color can unify an interior design throughout a house. The same color theme used throughout the house helps integrate interior spaces, even if adjoining rooms have different design styles. A chosen color can be used in the carpet of one room, then used in the vinyl or ceramic tile floor of another room to continue a common look throughout.

Dark floors can absorb an enormous amount of light, making a room look smaller and darker than necessary. Dark hardwood floors can be redone with glossy polyurethane to brighten up the room.

An effective floor pattern need not vie for attention—it can simply provide a background for other expressions of taste. You may want to add contrast by giving the floor a border. If the border is wide, the flooring itself becomes a separate area with the border serving as a transition to it.

*A **big bold** checkered pattern, set at a diagonal to the door, creates a striking effect is this early American entryway. A wide band of the same soft yellow used on the walls frames the vibrant floor design. This dramatic design creates an area that functions visually like a large area rug.*

Cool blue *is the theme of this ultra-contemporary kitchen. It hosts a custom-designed resilient floor that bursts onto the scene in bold geometric designs. Slick black ceramic countertops and sparking chrome fixtures reinforce the futuristic look of this electrifying kitchen.*

Photo courtesy of Mannington Mills Inc.

(right) **Bold and beautiful,** this black-and-white geometric pattern takes center stage in the design scheme of this kicky kitchen. Neutral white and black countertops, cupboards and chairs float serenely above the busy pattern in the floor. Accents of bright yellow and red are sprinkled throughout in the form of napkins, candles and cooking utensils.

(left) *A soft two-tone* pattern winds its way from the kitchen to the dining area, then down a hallway. The muted rosy hues of the colors add warmth and visually unify the large space. The white trim used on the walls and the cupboards is reflected in a faint grid pattern created by the resilient tiles.

Photo courtesy of Congoleum Corporation

Brightly colored *stains are used in a unique way on this plank flooring to create an exciting new look for hardwood floors. The random, uneven use of colors gives the floor a vibrant look and a sense of texture. Neutral colors and subdued shades are used in the furniture, walls and window treatments to keep interest focused on the floor.*

Small green accent tiles are used with larger white tiles to form a dainty diamond pattern across this bathroom floor. The fresh-looking floor pattern is reflected in the color and scale of the flowery stenciled design that winds around the bathtub and up across the walls.

DESIGN

Pattern & Scale

The pattern and scale of a flooring material combine with the existing surface textures and colors to create the final look of a room. Again, simplicity is the key to good design when working with pattern and scale. Large patterns will decrease the apparent size of a room, especially if the pattern contains several colors. Busy patterns distract from other design elements, and may make it harder to change the room in the future.

Scale refers to the proportional relationships of design elements. It is especially important when dealing with single units, like tiles or stones. The relationship between the size of tile or stone units, the width of grout lines and the size of the room must be carefully planned so the floor pattern will be proportional and visually balanced in the room.

The shapes that make up the pattern also affect the overall feeling of the design: curved shapes create a swirl of motion, angular shapes oppose and hold each other in place, geometric shapes combine with each other to form an integrated field. Keep these principles in mind whenever you are selecting patterns to help you choose those that are in harmony with your overall design.

Large floor areas can accommodate a larger-scaled pattern without overwhelming the room. But a small room, such as a bathroom, needs a simple pattern of smaller scale if the floor is to create a pleasant visual effect.

Photo courtesy of Armstrong World Industries

(left) ***A fanciful butterfly-shaped*** *design is used within a soft grid pattern that runs across this resilient floor. A stencil pattern incorporating the same butterfly motif floats across the wall just under the windowsill.*

(below) ***A beautifully polished*** *hardwood floor bucks tradition with colored stains and alternating planking patterns. The muted pastel decor makes this stylish, sophisticated floor design the focal point of the room.*

Photo courtesy of ENCURACOLOR Hardwood Flooring, Inc.

Photo courtesy of Congoleum World Industries

Realistic texture and coloring give the resilient flooring in this country-style kitchen the look and eye-catching appeal of an old-fashioned brick floor, but this durable alternative is more comfortable, easier to maintain and less expensive than the actual material.

DESIGN

Texture

Texture is often incorporated as part of the pattern. An embossed texture in the pattern highlights and defines the pattern more than a smooth surface. You can also use texture to more practical advantages. For rooms such as kitchens, bathrooms, laundry rooms and entryways, where the floor may get wet, the flooring material should have enough texture to prevent slipping.

Texture can also affect a room's ambience. For instance, a stone floor in a small, dark room may feel cool and inviting in the desert states, but more like a chilly dungeon in cold northern areas. When flooring materials change from room to room you can retain a unified design by keeping the color consistent and changing just the texture or material—for example, use a ceramic tile for the kitchen floor, and a carpet of the same or similar color in an adjoining room.

Photo courtesy of Amtico Company Limited. Photo opposite page courtesy of Florida Tile Industries, Inc.

A montage of textures, shapes, colors and seafaring creatures creates a watery theme for this one-of-a-kind bathroom. Custom-cut, high-quality vinyl is combined with actual beach pebbles, seashells and even a starfish to give this bathroom the look and feel of an authentic seaside setting. Even the bathtub seems seaworthy.

A PORTFOLIO OF

FLOORING
IDEAS

Photo courtesy of Florida Tile Industries, Inc.

HALLWAYS & ENTRYWAYS

An entryway is the place you receive callers; it gives people their first impression of your home. Hallways are thoroughfares linking the different areas of a house. Since hallways and entryways tend to be primarily floor, the material you choose will have a very strong impact on the design of the space.

Entryway, hallway and stairway floors should be coordinated so they make smooth transitions from one area of the house to another. You do not necessarily need to use the same floor covering throughout the house, but materials should be planned so the colors, textures and tones make a visual connection.

Many hallways are designed to be viewed from a stairway or landing above to showcase the stunning design created in a flooring treatment. These aerial views are framed by the shape and parameters of the hallway or entryway.

Hallways and entryways are usually high-traffic areas; they should be capable of taking a great deal of wear and tear. The surface should be tough, easy to clean, safe and nonslip, as well as good-looking.

Fortunately there are any number of flooring materials that meet all of these requirements. Traditional treatments for hallways are polished wood, tile, marble and stone slabs. Natural stone materials are expensive, but in the long run they last longer and offer a better choice of color, texture and pattern. Less expensive alternatives include realistic-looking imitations of marble and other natural stone, cork, ceramic tile, even hardwood, in the form of resilient floor tiles or sheeting. Resilient flooring is soft, warm and easier to install, and it makes an excellent choice for designing stylish hallways and entryways.

Marbleized ceramic *floor tiles, with colors and textures resembling hardwood flooring, are a smarter choice than real hardwood for this high-traffic entry area. The warm natural tones tie in visually with the soft beige color of the carpet on the stairway and in the living room area seen at the end of the hallway.*

Simplicity and sophistication *set the tone in this formal foyer. Majestic green and beige marble squares spread across the floor, forming an open checkerboard pattern. The long-lasting beauty of the marble ensures that this entryway will maintain its elegant appeal for many years to come.*

Clean, colorful *ceramic tiles are a clever floor covering for this inspired entryway. A subtle tile design creates the effect of an angled area rug that greets people as they enter the room. Small, glossy colored tiles that match the look of the larger tiles on the wall are interspersed throughout the floor design.*

An inspired inlaid design *gives guests a dramatic greeting in this elegant entryway. The only thing more impressive than the intricate beauty of this design is the strength and durability of the resilient material itself. Resistant to the rough treatment that is expected in an entryway, this material keeps its good looks for a very long time.*

(above) **New technology** in carpet fibers has expanded the role of carpeting. It is now a viable flooring material in more areas of the home than ever before. Still not the best choice for heavily trafficked areas, carpeting is a fine choice for this side entrance that sees a minimal amount of wear and tear.

(left) **The beauty** of this hardwood hallway floor is protected by a sturdy wool Dhurrie area rug. The durable wool rug acts as a buffer between the floor and the damaging dirt and debris brought in from the adjoining outdoor deck.

The smooth, weathered look of slate provides a rustic foundation for this southwestern-style setting. The deep color and uneven texture of real stone is authentically reproduced in durable, affordable, versatile vinyl—a warmer, more comfortable copy of the real thing.

Photo courtesy of Bruce Hardwood Floors

LIVING ROOMS & FAMILY ROOMS

The living room is the decorative center of a home. It is the part of the house we spend the most money on in order to represent and reflect our taste and style. As a personal showcase, the living room has the best furniture and the most sensational flooring. Since the floor constitutes one of the largest decorative elements in the room, the wrong choice could ruin the effect of the entire scheme.

These days, living rooms also double as family rooms, playrooms or dens, and the elements, particularly the floor, must satisfy more than one function. A combination of materials can be used to define and separate different areas of a room. This works best when the contrast isn't too extreme: for example, a hard surface butted onto a soft one but with the same color, pattern or design.

Take care when visually dividing a small room. To create the impression of space, it is best to use one type of flooring throughout and rely on a variety of lighting effects to change the emphasis according to the room's use.

The most popular floor treatment for living rooms is carpeting. Carpeting offers a way to harmonize and contrast color, pattern, style and texture with the furniture in a room. The cut of the pile determines a carpet's texture. The challenge is to balance the texture of the carpet with any textured upholstery fabrics, flat or glossy paints, wallpaper and other elements of the room's design. Carpeting is available in most colors from vivid primary and fashion colors to the natural wool shades, which have a pleasing fleck that helps hide dirt. Neutral carpet is perfect for rooms where you want to add an accent with special rugs or designer furniture.

The polished, clean style of ceramic tile is no longer limited to bathrooms and kitchens. Large, cream-colored textured tile supports the sunny southwestern style of this abode and gives the room a cool, comfortable feeling.

Photo left courtesy of Armstrong World Industries Inc.

Photo right courtesy of Congoleum Corporation

The flexibility of vinyl *makes it fun and functional. This tough, resilient material can be custom cut and installed to create almost any design imaginable. Here a family room floor is splashed with colorful geometric designs; the bold pattern on the floor balances the busy gingham upholstery and the brightly colored floral curtains. The light, neutral tones of the walls and floor help maintain a sense of calmness and space amongst the colorful chaos of this friendly fireplace area.*

Fun and functional, this high-gloss vinyl floor boasts the classic look of a traditional ceramic tile floor, but with the easy care and comfort of vinyl. The art deco diamond design adds a dash of color, updates the traditional styling of the space, and helps make a smooth transition from the den area to the kitchen.

The warm richness *of a polished hardwood floor becomes an elegant setting for this luxurious music room.*

(top) **Long, flowing lines** of this polished hardwood floor maximize the length of the room, while the hardwood flooring provides a durable, distinguished-looking surface.

(right) **Deep blue wall-to-wall carpet** brings soft comfort to this family room. A contrasting rectangle of lighter blue, with a diagonal texture, lightens the look of the dark blue carpet and creates the impression of an area rug in the center of the room.

(top) **A brilliantly colored,** custom-designed sculpted area rug makes quite a statement within the quiet calmness of this all-white living room. Brightly colored throw pillows add a dash of color to the couch and coordinate with the colors in the rug.

(bottom) **Rich red velvet** in the decor of this living room creates a regal appeal that is reflected in the custom design of the plush area rug. The polished hardwood floor underneath helps the room maintain an air of dignity and formality.

Photo courtesy of Phifer Wire Products, Inc.

Photo courtesy of Kolbe & Kolbe

Photo courtesy of Marvin Wndows

(top) Fiber flooring from the Far East—
*a Persian area rug with a Kashan design (near),
and one with a Bidjar pattern, from India (far),
maintain high profiles on the high-gloss, hardwood
beauty of this living room floor.*

(bottom) Velvety softness *radiates from the thick,
plush wall-to-wall carpet in this lavish living room.
Lush textures and a rich, cream color scheme
coordinate to create optimum elegance.*

Photo courtesy of Rushman Industries

Photo courtesy of Florida Tile Industries, Inc.

KITCHENS & DINING AREAS

In a kitchen, the floor takes more punishment than any other surface in the room. It must be able to withstand grease, water, heat, the weight of appliances and the concentrated wear of feet repeatedly standing in one spot or traveling over the same route between appliances and storage areas. Kitchen flooring must be resistant to stains, easy to clean, durable and nonslip for safety. Despite these rigid requirements, the flooring materials available today offer enough imaginative design ideas to meet everyone's needs.

The dining room used to be a room reserved for entertaining or having a formal dinner. In recent years, dining rooms have begun changing their purpose and their design, frequently sharing floor space with the kitchen, family room or living room. A successful flooring surface for this area must now combine the tough practical properties necessary for a kitchen floor with the more decorative needs of a dining room floor. It must be resistant enough to handle spills, yet complement the ambiance created in the dining area.

One solution to this dilemma is to choose a flooring that can be used in both the kitchen and the dining area. Hardwood, ceramic floor tiles or resilient flooring are materials that look great and can take the punishment a kitchen floor endures.

The other alternative is to break the room into separate, smaller areas by using different flooring materials for each area of the room. Such contrasting floor treatment serves to define the boundaries and different functions of the two areas. In smaller rooms, it is more effective to use materials that are visually harmonious, in order to make the overall space seem larger.

Photo courtesy of Florida Tile Industries, Inc.

The powdery soft brown *color and crisp, clean, white grout lines give a contemporary twist to the southwestern styling of this ceramic tile floor. The smooth feel of ceramic adds an air of elegance and keeps the room cool and comfortable, a big plus in warm weather.*

(below) **Rough-and-ready** *resilient tiles add a festive flair to this informal dining area. The soft textured pattern on the surface of the tiles can be seen when light reflects off the polished surface.*

(below) **The stately elegance** *of natural stone is authentically reproduced in this stunning state-of-the-art resilient floor. A thin line of brick red outlines the random design, while alternating shades of gray add depth and interest to an already incredible kitchen floor.*

Photo right courtesy of Amtico Company Limited

Photo left courtesy of Mannington Mills Inc.

Contemporary neoclassic decor is enhanced by the muted monotone colors of this kitchen and dining area. The resilient sheet vinyl flooring used here has a subtle texture for added safety and a soft tan color that brings out the natural beauty and warmth of the wood in the room.

The icy-cool look of a glass block wall is mirrored in the high-gloss vinyl floor of this kitchen. Designer styling in resilient flooring offers dynamic new looks like the exceptional beauty of the imitation marble shown here.

Resilient flooring gives a command performance in this distinguished dining room. Optimum elegance is achieved at a reasonable cost by installing resilient sheet flooring instead of the actual wood and marble materials depicted in the flooring design. The large grid pattern gives the floor substantial presence, balancing the dynamic look of the art deco decor.

The fresh, delicate *designs in this resilient flooring bring the garden indoors to this delightful dining area. A petite pastel pattern atop glossy white tile squares adds a dash of color, yet helps keep the room looking bright and breezy.*

The look of a real stone floor, *but softer to stand on. Hard wearing resilient flooring is soft underfoot compared to real marble, and won't crack or chip under normal kitchen conditions.*

Photo courtesy of Armstrong World Industries Inc.

(left) **Bold colors in this bright white kitchen** *are coordinated for high impact. Vibrant vinyl flooring colors can be cut to almost any custom design.*
(below) **A beautiful combination** *of elegant design and durability creates a fashionable, functional floor in this carefree kitchen. This floor delivers the satiny-smooth look of an authentic marble surface, but with the versatility of vinyl.*

Photo courtesy of Congoleum Corporation

(top) **The intriguing allure** of translucent quartz gives an upscale look to this distinctive dining room floor.

(bottom right) **A bold, geometric** checkerboard design adds interest without overpowering and sets the tone for this contemporary white country kitchen. Zesty reds and yellows add vivid accents in the form of ceramic ware and cooking utensils.

(bottom left) **Black lacquer** and polished hardwood cabinetry combine to create an ultrasleek contemporary kitchen. Resilient flooring offers the look of wood, with the ease of vinyl. Thin black pinstripes put a finishing touch on a fabulous-looking floor that won't warp, crack or splinter, even if it gets wet.

Photo courtesy of Bruce Hardwood Floors

(above) **The long-lasting beauty** of wood is the natural choice to showcase this traditional kitchen.

(left) **Real wood** and faux marble vinyl tiles combine to create a sturdy, carefree kitchen floor.

Photo courtesy of Amtico Company Limited

Photo courtesy of AlliedSignal Fibers

BEDROOMS

Bedrooms are quiet, personal places where the wear and tear on a floor is usually minimal. This is the room where you can splurge on the extravagant rugs or thick pile carpet. The main criteria for bedroom flooring is that it be warm and comfortable on bare feet.

Often, the style of bedroom furniture or the architecture of the house will set the decorative theme for the bedroom. Bedroom styles can be plush and luxurious, with thick pile carpet, or simple and provincial, with polished or bleached wooden floors. Your choice of flooring in the bedroom can set a mood or reinforce a theme. You can dress it up or down, according to taste and whim.

Marble or tile floors in a bedroom wouldn't be a practical choice, since no one wants to touch their feet down on cold stone first thing in the morning, but a similar look can be achieved with resilient flooring reproductions.

And any kind of hard surface can be softened with mats and rugs positioned where they will be needed most. Rugs and mats are the perfect accessories to help emphasize a design style: a soft area rug with a floral pattern of pink and gray for a bedroom that is decorated in buttons and bows, or Japanese bamboo or grass mats to enhance a simple Oriental theme.

Vinyl flooring is a good choice for children's bedrooms. It is soft, warm and flexible, but it's also durable and easy to clean. Equally warm and comfortable, and durable enough for a small child's room, are cork tiles.

The earthy tones and weathered look of this ceramic tile floor give charm to this Victorian-style bedroom. The smooth, cool stone creates a tranquil backdrop for this restful retreat. The timeless appeal of ceramic ensures that this floor will complement almost any decor.

(top) **The warmth** *of a hardwood floor enhances the charm of this country bedroom. The plank flooring has exposed wood plugs in a contrasting color that create the look of a much older floor.*

(bottom left) **Comfortable and warm** *underfoot, the vinyl in this cozy country bedroom is an earthy green color that blankets the floor like soft moss. A white rectangle design inset into the flooring creates the illusion of an area rug beneath the bed.*

(bottom right) **A woven cotton** *area rug provides softness and warmth underfoot and adds a splash of color to this child's bedroom. The painted hardwood floor is a soft eggshell white which makes the small room appear larger than it actually is.*

Vivid wood-grain texture adds a nice contrast to the quiet serenity of this restful bedroom. The warm beauty of natural wood is the perfect foil for other natural materials like wool and cotton linens. The texture of a natural wool throw rug adds softness and warmth to the glossy hardwood floor.

You can opt for wall-to-wall luxury when choosing bedroom carpeting. Bedroom floors don't have to take the punishment other floors do, so an expensive, luxurious look makes more sense here than anywhere else in the house. The soft, dusty-rose color of this plush carpet provides a warm, rich setting for the satiny decor of this bedroom.

(below) *A large Persian area rug,* bearing a traditional Sarouq design, brings warmth to this hardwood floor. The soft texture and warm colors brighten the heavy, dark feeling of the furniture.

Photo left courtesy of Devenco Products.   Photo right courtesy of AlliedSignal Fibers

Photo courtesy of Florida Tile Industries, Inc.

BATHROOMS

The smaller dimensions of a bathroom floor make it the perfect place to experiment with more extravagant, expensive materials and imaginative ideas. A bathroom doesn't have to be decorated in pastels; dramatic colors often are very effective and interesting in small rooms.

One way to visually increase the sense of space in a small room is to continue the flooring material up the walls. Choose plain or subtly patterned styles, and use borders and stripes to add highlights and points of interest.

Combining several flooring materials gives you the option of incorporating materials that aren't normally considered the most practical for a bathroom with other, more accepted bathroom flooring materials. An example would be combining carpeting and ceramic tile.

Natural stone like marble or terrazzo can also be incorporated into a bathroom's design

scheme this way. Limiting the area where the expensive stone is used reduces the cost and can be extremely effective when the stone is combined with the right materials.

As in the kitchen, the materials used in the bathroom must meet certain requirements before they are considered suitable. They must be safe and comfortable underfoot and completely resistant to water, splashes, steam, powder and oils. Among the suitable choices are: ceramic tiles, vinyl, even carpet or wood, if specifically prepared for this type of environment.

If you choose carpet for the bathroom, it is important to use a type specially designed to withstand steam and splashes. If ceramic or marble feel too cold, the designs available in resilient flooring let you re-create any flooring treatment imaginable. Resilient flooring feels soft and comfortable, and withstands splashes.

Neoclassic styling *in a soothing, watercolor pastel gives this bath an elegant feel. Matching ceramic wall tile is used on the counter, wall and tub enclosure to create a unified look and visually expand the sense of space in the room.*

Stylish design, *rugged durability and easy-care maintenance are just a few of the many attributes of this vinyl bathroom floor. The small diamond pattern creates a distinguished design that stands out against the bright white background.*

Purples and blues
form a lovely lavender theme and a serene bathroom setting. Fluffy white cotton area rugs and soft, sheer white curtains are the finishing touches for a look that fills this beautiful bathroom with a soft, springtime freshness.

If you want to step onto something more comfortable in your bathroom, consider the possibilities of a plush pile. Carpeting made specifically for bathrooms is designed to withstand steam and splashes. Manufactured in standard carpet color ranges, it can be matched to carpeting in connecting rooms or hallways.

Distinctive vinyl flooring adds a romantic flavor to the Egyptian accents in the room. The earthy brown tone and embossed texture re-create the image of ancient stone tiles.

La Petite Fleur is the design theme for the floor in this animated antique bathroom. The bright colors of the towels and curtain are reflected in the intricate design of the resilient floor.

The classic look *of rich stone tiles bathes this bathroom in a tranquil sea of green. The large raised tub is enclosed with bright white tiles that give the bath a crisp, fresh, clean appeal. Thin white lines on the floor form a pattern that reflects the sparkling white in the tub surround and mirrors the pattern formed by the decorative muntins in the windows.*

Photo courtesy of Florida Tile Industries Inc.

PORCHES & CONSERVATORIES

A harmonious transition is what you should strive for when choosing flooring for porches, conservatories and other areas that link the inside of your home to the outdoors.

Select a flooring material that looks good with the existing decor and will visually extend your living area into the yard or garden. It must also be weatherproof and tough. Materials designed for pathways and patios, like stone, brick and weather-treated wood, are ideal and come in a variety of shapes and colors.

Avoid carpeting. A porch or conservatory often acts as a buffer between the house and the outdoors, so the floor must be able to take extremely hard wear and yet be easy to clean.

Determine the function of your conservatory or porch and the practical limitations of certain types of flooring. A porch may need to house wet umbrellas, muddy shoes, roller skates and a wet dog. The flooring material you install here needs to be durable enough to take it all.

Once you know how the area will be used you can start exploring different creative options. Ceramic tile or natural stone floors are a luxurious and logical choice for these areas; they stand up to abuse and can soak up natural heat from the sun during the day and release it at night. Resilient flooring materials are also a good choice; they are extremely durable and can achieve the look of real stone without the coldness or the expense.

*A **custom-designed** vinyl floor beautifully imitates the rich look of natural wood. Resilient flooring is the smart choice as a more durable alternative to wood. Real wood flooring, particularly the inlaid border, could not handle the changes in temperature in this indoor/outdoor environment.*

The bold design of this atrium *sends the senses spinning. Metallics are incorporated into the custom design of this resplendent resilient floor. By combining the flooring pattern, the bold lines in the railing of the spiral staircase, and the ceiling lines of this atrium, the room achieves a visual sense of motion, heightened by the wonderfully wild design on the walls.*

(above) **Soft, brown squares** with the look of natural stone tiles combine with a French door that opens to the outside to create an outdoor feeling inside this sunny artist's studio. Versatile vinyl offers the perfect choice for an authentic-looking stone tile floor that's also comfortable and easy to clean.

(above) **Tightly woven** pile carpeting is a comfortable choice for this sunny solarium. A soft floral design in the carpet creates a small grid pattern that resembles a tiled floor and, when combined with the lush green plants, gives the room the look and feel of an outdoor patio.

(right) **The ox-blood coloring and shading** of natural brick is strikingly reproduced in the vinyl floor that lies in this sunny solarium.

LIST OF CONTRIBUTORS

We'd like to thank the following companies for providing the photographs used in this book:

ADO Corporation
P.O. Box 3447
Spartanburg, SC 29304
1-800-845-0918

AlliedSignal Fibers
2100 Fiber Park Drive
Dalton, GA 30720
1-800-441-8185

Andersen Window Corporation
Bayport, MN 55003
1-800-654-3008

The Amtico Company Limited
6480 Roswell Road
Atlanta, GA 30328
1-800-268-4260

American Olean Tile Company
1000 Cannon Avenue
Lansdale, PA 19446-0271
215-855-1111

Armstrong World Industries Inc.
P.O. Box 8022
Plymouth, MI 48170-9948
1-800-704-8000

Bruce Hardwood Floors
A Division of Triangle Pacific Corp.
16803 Dallas Parkway
Dallas, TX 75428
800-526-0308

Color Tile Inc.
515 Houston Street
Fort Worth, TX 76102
Over 800 Color Tile & Carpet locations coast to coast.
For the store nearest you, call 1-800-NEARBY YOU

Congoleum Corporation
3705 Quackerbridge Road - Suite 211
P.O. Box 3127
Mercerville, NJ 08619-0127
609-584-3000

Conrad Imports
575 Tenth Street
San Francisco, CA 94103-4829
415-626-3303

Crestline Windows & Doors
SNE Enterprises
One Wausau Center
Wausau, WI 54402-8007
715-845-1161

Devenco Products
2688 East Ponce De Leon Avenue
Decatur, GA 30030
1-800-888-4597

ENDURACOLOR
Hardwood Flooring, Inc.
1942 Tigertale Boulevard
Dania, Florida 33004
305-922-WOOD

Florida Tile Industries Inc.
P.O. Box 3900
Peoria, IL 61612
1-800-FLA-TILE

Hurd Millwork Company
P.O. Box 319
Medford, WI 54451
715-748-2011

Kolbe & Kolbe
1323 South 11th Avenue
Wausau, WI 54401
715-842-5666

Loewen Windows
Box 2260
Steinbach, Manitoba
Canada R0A2A0
204-326-6446

Mannington Resilient Floors
P.O. Box 30
Salem, NJ 08079-0030
609-935-3000

Marvin Windows & Doors
Warroad, MN 56763
1-800-346-5128

Phifer Wire Products, Inc.
P.O. Box 1700
Tuscaloosa, AL 35403-1700
1-800-633-5955

Rushman Industries
2929 Irving Boulevard
Dallas, TX 75247
214-943-1000

Spring Window Fashions
7549 Graber Road
Middleton, WI 53562-1096
1-800-356-9102